This one is special to me. I remember being in a place of bondage, where I didn't like myself, what I was doing or who I was with. I would borrow money from her; spend time at her house and sit up for hours talking about where I was mentally and in my relationships. One time I sat up in the middle of the night wondering if anybody cared or knew what was happening in me. Suddenly I saw this woman in the corner, I saw what she had on earlier in the morning and at that moment I listened to hear what she was saying. She was praying earnestly for me. I heard her say my name, I heard her crying out to God for me...That was the very first moment anyone has ever

ministered deliverance to me...and she wasn't in the room

This book is dedicated to my oldest sister Donna Bell...her continued prayer and supplication opened a door for me to be free!!!

Acknowledgements

Always a son. No matter where I go and what I do...I will always be a son. For this reason I celebrate the leadership and teachings of my parents Pastor Leon K. Shipman Sr. and Elect Lady Dian Shipman. Deliverance was never something that was new to them, and will never be something they are far away from, because they walk in authority.

My Senior Pastor, the Great Superintendent of the Freedom District...Dr. Darthanian Y.B. Nichols. He lets me be me. (Yes I upset him), but when it comes time to work...I believe and trust that he believes and trust we can do the work. Thank God for an apostolic leader in the life of this Prophet.

Drs. Jerry and Sherill Piscopo. The experiences that I have had and the biblical depth I have gained on deliverance and inner healing can never be explained in a sentence or a paragraph. The seeds they have sown in teaching, training and activation has been priceless. (They are technically my Uncle and Aunt).

The leaders of BCOM and WITS that have labored with me and fought with me in teachings, seminars and at the altar: Elder and Mother Broughton (my godparents), they know how to fight and war, Prophetess Nichole Bradford, my first protégé, is a beast and walks in kingdom authority. Pastor Parthinia, Missionary Christian, Minister Ben, Minister DeAndre, Pastor Chris, Minister

About the Author

Elder RayVon L. Shipman was born in Detroit, Michigan and was saved at age 9. During a revival, at age 12, he received the gift of the Holy Spirit. Soon after, he felt a call to the ministry. God spoke to him through Jeremiah, Chapter 1, and "he was called from his mother's womb, as a prophet." God used him to minister to adults and youth alike. God used many people during that time to mentor him including the pastor and leaders of New Christ Temple COGIC and his father, Pastor Leon K. Shipman. His father, Pastor Leon K. Shipman, Sr., began a ministry where Elder Ray served as a deacon for two years. He was also appointed to oversee the worship team, Sunday school, work with the youth group, finances, and even maintained the church in the absence of his parents. He was licensed to preach through the COGIC and continued to grow and develop.

After attending a deliverance seminar at Evangel Christian Churches, he felt the leading of the Lord to covenant with that ministry. For one year, he was faithful at his father's church and Evangel Christian Churches. Being released by his father from Walk In The Spirit he officially joined ECC. After joining, he came in covenant with Evangel Association of Churches and Ministries (EACM). He soon noticed many changes and an increase in his ministry. Because of the network of prayer, God began to speak clearly about his next step. After hearing the Lord speak, "roots down, fruit up, build another man's ministry," he took the position on staff as the Youth

Pastor and worked faithfully for 7 years. He was also an engineer on the radio, director of the drama department and worked as an assistant lead in the prophetic training, deliverance and inner healing teams.

He was ordained to the prophetic ministry and was offered the opportunity to pastor his own church called, Evangel Mt Clemens on Joy Blvd, in Mt Clemens. In a matter of 3 months, God increased the church from 12 to 60 people. God saw fit to reposition him again, and returned home to Walk In The Spirit COGIC, where he was ordained and began working with his father in ministry.

Life happened, and Prophet Ray left the ministry for a season but continued to try and find his footing in ministry and reconcile his personal issues. God saw fit for him to do a community event in which he was ministered to by Dr. Darthanian Nichols of Breaking Chains Outreach Ministries (BCOM). Within weeks, Prophet Ray, joined the ministry and committed whole heartedly to the vision of BCOM. Currently, He has earned his Bachelor's in Business Administration, is pursuing his MBA and works in ministry as the Assistant Pastor and Administrator of BCOM.

Ministry engagements can be set up by emailing at ray.shipman@yahoo.com and you can also find him on Facebook at RayVon Shipman.

"Crazy" Faith

Intro-

I grew up in the church. Literally. I was at each and every service…on time!!! I can probably count on one hand how many services I have missed purposely (even the accidental one's that I missed was probably done because I was at some other service). One of the things that remained consistent in my life and in every ministry, I have ever been a part of, is the life of the Gifts, fruit and the authority of God's presence and power.

To this day is rare for any person that I am connected to in ministry, to not, even accidently, end up doing something prophetic, deliverance, healing…something.

We grew up "pleading the blood". We grew up rebuking the devil. We knew what it meant to understand that demons and angels were real...we didn't have to be convinced, we saw them first hand.

The other thing we experienced was mental illness. Even though we didn't discuss it, it was pushed under a rug and ignored; it was just as real as the book you hold in your hand (or on your tablet). This was the issue, we weren't educated enough to discern the difference because they both looked alike. The demons screamed and the mentally ill person screamed. The mentally ill person seemed to blow up in the middle of service for no reason and so did the demon. We had no idea how to differentiate between the two. It wasn't until I got older, wiser and attained some education that I started piecing together this whole thing. Are we ministering to people in faith, or are we ministering to their crazy (not the technical term).

"Crazy" faith, will discuss the impact mental illness has had, is having and will have in the church, as well as the impact of deliverance. We will cover experiences, biblical principle, as well as steps for the person suffering with mental illness and demonic oppression to take in order for them to experience freedom, wholeness, recovery and healing.

Pay close attention; keep a note pad near you, because questions will be asked...you can always email me for information, because you're going to want answers.

P.Ray

CHAPTER 1
A Woman & Her Baby

So, this book will toggle between several different principles, definitions and experiences. I need you to keep an open mind and heart as I attempt to try and bring light to some of the things that we discuss here. Some will be funny but have a serious point to it, and I need you to be able to eat the meat and spit out the bones.

I had to be around the age of 7 or 8. Remember I grew up in the church, so we knew all the songs already, because we grew up in a traditional popular denomination. Our musician was the pastor's daughter. The drummer was the pastor's grandson; we taught bible study on regular Tuesday services so youth services were no big deal to us. We were in church all the live long day.

I remember our pastor preaching a sermon on demonology. Let me correct that a series on demonology. He had stuff printed out and we had folders and everything. Actually, the parents had all of that we were told that we shouldn't deal with stuff like this because we were too young.

Let me tell you right now, do not believe that garbage. I'm not trying to be unscrupulous, mean or attacking. They only did what they did in order to protect us, which in turn disabled us because we weren't prepared when it was time to battle the wiles of the devil, thus we had to learn on the job, making mistakes, avoiding friendly fire and not using discernment.

I would sneak and read the book throughout the week in order to try and keep up with what was being taught. It was very interesting to me. The study of angels and demons. The declaration of God's authority over everything and anything was eye opening and the fear instilled in us regarding the devil was terrifying.

This is the key issue. We were only educated regarding what other people were educated on. I had questions. I wanted to know what was happening, even as a child and I wasn't given the option of asking those questions, but started to have supernatural experiences. What am I supposed to do?

During one of these teachings, on a Friday evening around 10:30pm. Let me help you. We had pastoral teaching on Friday nights. It started at 7pm for prayer.

7:30 we went right into devotional and testimony service. You know, singing can't nobody do you like Jesus, for 45 minutes. Then from that everybody testified...EVERYBODY!!! We didn't really have lives so it was always the same testimony every single week.

We were just finishing up the teaching, and because we couldn't fall asleep in church either, we were wide awake and resistant participants with everything. A lady came in and sat in the back of the church and was quietly muttering to her and rocking back and forth. When I glanced to the back, I noticed that she had what appeared to be a baby blanket in her arms. I thought to myself, awwwww, she brought the baby to church.

I could hear the woman in the back starting to cry and whimper. I thought to myself again, that poor baby must be ill. After the bible study was done, there was no activation, but an altar call was given. The woman slowly got out of her seat with her baby wrapped snuggly in her blanket and said she wanted prayer for her baby. The baby wasn't eating right and wasn't sleeping throughout the evenings.

As they finally got up to the altar, she held her baby very close and wrapped in the blanket and presented the baby to the pastor. She slowly unwrapped the baby and as the head popped up, we noticed that the baby had white hair. I said to myself, what is that? It was a Jack-Russell terrier. People jumped back in awe and started "pleading the blood". I didn't know what to say about any of it. I just looked in awe as everyone prayed, extremely loudly. I couldn't figure out if they were praying for the dog or the woman. The pastor eventually put the woman out of the church. I always wondered what happened to that dog.

Clearly, we have someone acting in extreme faith or that's just mentally ill...or the lay term would be crazy. Honestly, I pray for my pets now too...so I don't see the problem. They've been to the church, sang with us for worship rehearsal. Let everything that has breathe...

What is missed in this story is the exploration of the ministry team to respond to a demon. Was there something demonic happening...possibly. Was there a woman in need there, obviously? The inability for us to discern when there is a mental illness and when there is a demon manifesting, comes from our ignorance on both ends. A gentle understanding of demonic activity and simple psychology won't make you a therapist, social worker or demon slayer. What it will do, is activate the wisdom that's already in you so that you will respond appropriately to what is in front of you, versus what people have taught you is crazy or demonic.

Growing up doing ministry...not just in church I saw varied things that now I understand as crazy. Please excuse my use of the word crazy, I know it can be seen as offensive so we will interchangeably use it with mentally ill and mental illness. I mean no offense whatsoever, just taking writing liberties. That woman that was always at the altar going through "purging", something we call deliverance now, may have been a mixture of demonic activity as well as mental illness.

Do I believe in demonic activity...absolutely and we will get into more of that in a few. I also understand we are humans that can have chemical imbalances that manifest in major depressive disorders, psychoaffective disorders and a host of other disorders. To eliminate the stigma, it's kind of like having acid reflux, something isn't working right.

The issue is not just about demonic activity or about mental illness, but the balance of the two. It's amazing to me how we can and have chosen to focus specifically on one particular area, which actually makes sense. We are supposed to be a spiritual hub. We are the spiritual super power in the earth. But while Jesus was here he ministered to the whole man. As the church, it should be our job to do exactly the same thing and not do one and leave the other undone. It is our job to employ and refer people that have recurring symptoms that appear to be demonic, to a mental health professional.

If someone has a heart attack in the middle of your service, do you lay hands and pray and keep preaching or do you lay hands and pray while someone calls 911. The balance of the two is what is necessary.

The bible tells us in Romans that we should be renewing our minds. Making new again and continually. The bible says in Colossians that we have the mind of Christ. Using both of these scriptures we already have success in bringing our mind and thoughts captive to the obedience of Christ, but scripture goes on to tell us that we should confess our faults one to another. What do I associate that with? THERAPY!!! Talk to someone. There will be pastors that are reading this that suffer from depression, but won't talk to anybody about it because they are the "pastor". Nobody cares if you're dead. The fact is you are needed here and we can't produce is you are not planting seeds.

I remember a pastor that we used to fellowship with years ago had a church right down the street from my parent's church. He was a prominent minister in the area. He was one of those megaphone preachers. Stood on the street, had a television show and very controversial. He'd preached for my dad's church a time or two; I thought he was a pretty cool guy. One day while walking home from school, we saw the police in front of his church. We were all gathering for bible study. His people were showing up, we were all very concerned. My dad went to see what was happening and came back in tears. This pastor had parked in the back of his church and taken a gun and shot himself in the head.

How did these prophetic people miss this? How did we miss the fact that he was so consumed with all that was going on in his life, ministry and world that he felt he had no more hope but to kill himself. We aren't going to get into the whole debate about if he went to heaven or hell (I don't believe that suicide is sin, there I said it. The person that does damage to themselves, clearly are not in their right mind and needs to be ministered to, in therapy and medication. I can't see justice being torment on earth and torment for eternity. I don't know how God does it but I am convinced his grace finds a way to rebuild that person's mind...)

The depression must be overwhelming to pastors and people in ministry that give their lives, finances and time to people who sometimes seem to not care about anything that they have to offer or sacrifice. The feelings of being alone, unheard, ignored and just plain ole disrespected are things that just don't go away, especially in a setting like the church. Respect the Judge, not the pastor. Respect the teacher, not the pastor. Respect the traffic laws, but not the one who is the watchman for your soul…that's witchcraft and control. Have a seat and get set free. I'm not sure where we get any of that from.

I'm not saying that our pastors and leaders suffer from depression because of us, but we may not help much either. Mental illness is a serious problem in the church, not because we ignore it, but because we typically say it's a demon. That thinking by itself would be diagnosed as someone who is religiously preoccupied.

I am not credentialed to diagnose anyone officially. I have worked in the mental health field for over 10 years. I have worked helping to diagnose people, in the inpatient and outpatient field. I have also been working in ministry for 26 years. I have lots of experience in both sides. The one thing that can be confirmed is the fact that we have overlooked a group of people that need more than just prayer, tongues and a preached word.

I know that there are going to be people that are going to argue my point, but I challenge you to look around your church and see how many people right now are living in a place of cycled depression and they have lived at the altar. They have fallen on the floor, gone through deliverance and have not gotten a break through. How about get them away from the altar and then get them into treatment with therapy and a psychiatrist. Some will argue that we shouldn't need that. Jesus had a doctor on His team, so why wouldn't you put a doctor on His team too? It just makes sense. The bible tells us that we should confess, talk about or admit our faults one to another. This is what I like to call THERAPY.

For whatever reason we consider it a bad thing to talk to someone who goes to a therapist. I have no idea why? You're always calling me, talking to pastor or bothering some minister with your problems. The fact is Jesus is the great counselor, not us. If they aren't experienced in counseling and therapy, I would suggest reaching out to someone outside that has experience in building you mentally and emotionally and leaving the ministry stuff to the church.

Now, this is the thing too. We also need to understand that there are some things that are completely demonic as well. There was a woman I know, that used to come into the clinic I worked at. She was outpatient for the most part but she hit a really hard area in life and was brought inpatient. She was not comfortable with that at all. It actually seemed to make her worst by being inpatient. The lady could be heard sometimes praying in her room throughout the day, so I knew that she was "spiritual".

She didn't sleep throughout the evening, (I worked midnights), so I knew during the "witching hour" she was tormented the most. I would watch as she went to groups, talked to the doctor and took medications. Nothing seemed to relieve her of the torment that she was experiencing.

One evening I flat out asked her what she was afraid of. I know your question is: Why would you ask about fear, when she is depressed and tormented. The bible says that fear torments in 1 John 4:18, but perfect loves casts out all fear. So, I asked her if I could pray for her. I prayed and cast out the demon of fear that would torment her. I prayed and asked God to release on her the garment of praise. She lifted her hands and praised God softly. That was all I needed, because I believed the word of the Lord. For the spirit of heaviness he gave the garment of praise. Within days she was released and never came back.

In this case, she was being tormented by a demonic spirit, no amount of therapy or drug helped. I suggested to her that she still go to therapy until she feels comfortable, but the tormenting spirit had lifted. How did I know it worked? She went right to sleep after we prayed. We watched a person that was tormented and couldn't sleep suddenly be able to sleep and rest.

There was another woman who came into the clinic who was nonresponsive. I looked at her and knew without any words or trying to figure it out, I discerned that she was demonically controlled. There was a demon that needed to be cast out of her…period. We can do medicine and therapy all day and that's not going to work. Clearly, it didn't work because she's not inpatient.

There was a coworker that understood what I saw and agreed to get me in to see her and minister to her. She had been non responsive for about 3 months, not talking, no moving, no eating nothing. Let me tell you. I got into that room with my coworker. He started praying in the Holy Ghost and I spoke directly to that demon and called that thing out. There wasn't' much response except for her eyes. She looked at me with this void in her eyes, when we started praying and as we prayed for her, this rage came through. As we ministered to her we spoke to her and asked her if she would hear us and asked if she wanted to get out of the wheel chair and back to her life. She started to tear up and suddenly there was a blink behind her eyes, a flicker of life and hope. She wanted to be free. I prayed and declared the freedom of Christ on that woman and left for the day.

I came into work the next day and she was walking to the lunch room for breakfast. My friend and co-worker looked at each other and smiled as the rest of the staff looked in awe. The day after that she wanted to take a shower and speak to someone. The family was called and wanted to know what we had done in order to get her to talk. By the third day she was able to come up to me and give me a hug (in appropriate in this field but...) and say she remembers everything and felt like she was trapped in herself. Thanks for being sensitive to God and helping me get free.

In tears I looked at her as she WALKED away of her own accord and celebrated the freedom of Christ in her.

Sometimes we see the result of demonic activity in our lives after the demonic cycle has started. After the cycle has started then we need to be mended and delivered. It takes all of it! We are Spirit, soul and body. We have to understand that we need freedom and deliverance and hope, and help and encouragement. Throughout this book we will explore several different experiences, biblical references, clinical theories and testimonials. The entire purse is not to just get caught up in one area but to find the balance of all of it.

Remember the story about the woman and her dog? I believe that part of the reason that she was able to come in was because the ground was fertile for freedom. What does that mean? I think that the fact that we were already studying angels and demons made us sensitive to demonic activity. It's kind of like rubbing your hair with the balloon, increasing the magnetism.

Just as the word declares that as we praise God, he inhabits our praise. I am a believer in the fact that the things we study and learn are the things that we become accountable for. Nobody finds it amazing that when we start teaching about finances, people give more? When you teach on healings, people get sick, so that healings can take place. When you teach about angels and demons, freedom and deliverance, suddenly the faith level of people gets elevated and they are held liable for the things that they now have seen and heard and now they have to deal with what happens and comes along with that teaching.

As it pertains to this chapter and this book, you are now responsible for finding the balance of the two. Deliverance and the practical side of the person that needs ministry as well. Do not be pushed into a super spiritual bondage and ignore the necessary place you need to be in order to minister to the whole man. Religiosity will say if they can't get free from a word, they need to fast, if the fasting doesn't work, they need to pray, if the prayer doesn't work…and the list will continue.

Humanism says get into therapy and on medication and you should be fine. Do the work and you will recover? Truth is the reason why there are so many issues in the church is because we have not dealt with the demonic issues, we have not dealt with the chemical imbalances, we also have not deal with the emotional stance, nor have we dealt with the responsibilities of our own stuff.

Everything is not demonic, everything is not God...some things are a result of consequences of our actions.

CHAPTER 2
Can't Be Honest...Can't be Saved

Can't be honest...can't be saved is a saying that I heard when I first started attending my church. At first I didn't really understand it but gathered a lot of wisdom from it as I continued to grow in my own deliverance. The truth of deliverance is not just about the authority of casting out a demon, but it is about being honest about your struggle. It is about being honest about your own personal bondage.

As we explore more about deliverance the importance of taking responsibility for our own issues. This is not about blaming the devil. We have ministered to so many people that have been at the altar and gone home and tried to figure out why they keep ending up in the same area of bondage.

Let me help you with that answer, the issue is not the devil...the issue is you, lol. We can say all day that I need to be free from this spirit or this bondage, which is probably true, but the real issue is that you don't want to be. How do I know? Even when he sets you free from the bondage that has kept you tied up for several years, as soon as you get off the floor at the church, talk to your friends at church, jump in the car and head home, you pick up the phone and call what's his name and redo the bondage you were just freed from.

The issue in this section is that it's not about demons. It's about your responsibility in your freedom. We can be so focused on the demonic realm that we forget that we have our own responsibilities in maintaining freedom. Try not opening a door for demonic attack. If you want to really be free, stop putting yourself into the place to be bound.

It's really as simple as that. I know many are reading already thinking but I can't help it. But you can. The bible says in Galatians that the fruit of the spirit is love, joy, peace, longsuffering, gentleness, meekness and temperance. Temperance is self-control. The reason that I have the ability to not fall into bondage is because I have the Holy Spirit and the Holy Spirit gives me self-control I don't have to end up in bondage because I have control over myself and realize that I am sensitive to His Spirit when He says, don't go here, don't do this, don't associate with that one.

Realize that our options are simple. We already have the victory over the enemy, the only way we can be defeated by the enemy is when we give up our God given authority to someone or something else; or even to a person.

We have a responsibility to maintaining our authority and our deliverance. It is one of the most annoying things in the entire world, to minister to someone in the area of deliverance and the moment they get tempted they are right back in that place. You don't want to be free. Admit the truth of that thing. Now, it's a different thing when you have been resisting the enemy have submitted to God and still end up in that bondage. Yes, then it's a deliverance issue.

God has shown us in scripture how we are to maintain our victory and authority. Scripture shows us that we have already overcome the world. How do we always keep getting defeated? How do we always end up in bondage? We have given our responsibility to the enemy. This is what I mean: What am I supposed to do with my addiction to going to the club? I know somebody will say that it's not an addiction, but your responses to being told you shouldn't go or that you need to take some time away from the club, is that of an addict that is being told they need to go into treatment. It's met with resistance.

The person that suffers with depression doesn't have the easiest time pulling themselves out. I understand the feeling. What I also understand is that before I start to spiral downward, I have that time when I can put on the garment of praise versus, wallowing in my depression and enjoying the feeling of depression.

Many people will say that they can't help but feel depressed, of course, I understand the feeling, but either we believe the word of the Lord or not. This is where we miss Victory. We believe in the word when it is ok, when victory is seen in the times when we have little to no one to rely on and trust. I have been going over and over in my mind, how to be successful in my relationship with God and truth is, it's trusting His word. It's not in the shout (which is good), it's not in the going to church (which is a must), but none of that is going to equate victory until you put to work the word that has been spoken and that you already know.

Let's explore some other issues: I need deliverance from over eating. Drive past the fast food joint and cook a meal. When you realize how much money you have spent eating and how much you have to do in order to eat as much as you have been at a fast food joint.

I have trouble with my mouth and I can't help it when I get angry to go off on people. You need the Holy Ghost. I just told somebody else the other day that you may lie to the judge, but don't like to yourself!!! My cousin used to always tell me, to thine own self be true. Don't lie to yourself.

The bible shows us that when we are tempted we are pulled and drawn to it by our own lusts and desires. This means that it's something that we really are attracted to and want to do. I can NEVER be tempted to slip into drugs. It's never been something that has been enticing to me. But you put something else in front of me that I have enjoyed before then you will see how I have to struggle to resist it. But my ability to submit to God and resist the devil is victory for me. It only comes with my ability to submit to what His word says. I have to make the choice to do what He says to do; therefore I will have the victory over myself and over the enemy.

Continue in prayer and the word is the other thing. It is our responsibility to grow and increase in the kingdom. Just like if you never eat or drink food, you will be malnourished and eventually die. The same thing goes for us in the spirit. It is our responsibility (not the pastors), to maintain a healthy diet spiritually.

In Acts the church of Berea were MORE blessed because they went back to search and see if the things that were preached were true. This is your job!!! Not your friend or the prophet that comes in from out of town. It's your job to spend time with God, in His word and in his presence. I challenge you to take responsibility for your own freedom and deliverance. As we continue to get into this book we will discover what more responsibilities we have in getting, maintain and standing in deliverance.

Humility is also the key. In our pursuit of freedom and deliverance, we have got to learn that we are not the ones in charge. But, yielding to His grace and mercy will set us up to be at a place to not rely on our own strength but on His. By grace are you saved…Sozo. That's the Greek word for salvation. That means saved or salvation from the inside out. Our salvation is not just about us not going to hell and going to heaven, but in living a life of abundance and freedom in our relationship with God.

CHAPTER 3
Pre-Deliverance

Let's answer some questions surrounding deliverance:

I am a born again, spirit filled, blood washed tongue talking, operating in the prophetic, laying hands and seeing sick people healed believer...how or why would I need deliverance?

Ok, take a deep breath and walk through this with me. I believe that all of us need deliverance. Once we come to Jesus we are set free from the bondage of the enemy and the snares that would entrap us, that would cause us to fall into the pit of hell. We have been set free from the control of the devil and his principalities. But, we still need deliverance. Our spirits have been quickened and made alive, our souls and bodies need to be delivered. I know, I know somebody is already trying to put this together and figure out how this is even biblical. I'm going to take you there.

Think about this. When you got saved, did you ever get sick? Have you known a believer that has died from cancer or some other physical ailment? That's because when sin entered the world all of this other stuff entered as well.

Continued heart break, the cycle of bad relationships and accepted abuse are all branches that stem from the tree of bondage and the demonic realm. Deliverance is freedom from the bondage and control of the enemy in our soul or physical body.

The soul is the seat of our emotions, will and or mind. This is where those buttons are always being pushed. This is the where we are sitting in our houses alone and suddenly have a fleeting thought about someone and we are now angry about something that happened several years ago.

That's the cycle of the enemy and a place of bondage. We aren't just going to talk about demonic possession, oppression or whatever verbiage we want to use. We are going to explore deliverance from cycles, principalities powers and rulers of darkness of this world.

Remember the story of Job. The thing that we always remember is the fact that Job had everything taken away from him. We think about his family and him having sores. We preach about how God allowed it to happen stating that Job was an upright man, and he was tempted because God knew that he would stand.

The truth is in that first chapter, it tells us why the enemy had the ability to do all that he did to Job. He was able to do that because of one simple thing. We actually discussed it earlier. Job was tormented and torment comes from...fear. The bible says that Job went and did several sacrifices, for his kids, just in case because he feared. Go back and read it and search it out and see what it says. The fact is that we give the devil a foothold to do some of the things to us.

How do you give the devil a foot hold and what exactly is that? If you have ever seen someone climb a mountain, the only way that they can do it is to start with a foothold. They have to get at a place where they can find stability in their footing, a place where they can get in and pull themselves up. We set up a foothold in our lives by several things. When we are given the chance to forgive, and we choose to not, this is a foothold.

As I am writing this it took a minute to step back and see how much I wanted to share. I was in prayer talking to God about this and he clearly said that I was going to have to tell part of my story. Get Ready!!!

When it comes to responsibility I had to realize that some of the behaviors that I indulged in were not demons. I went through deliverance. I went through inner healing. I went through travail, crying out, seeking God for 7 days, fasting and prayer and still...my flesh was out of control. It wasn't until I took the resolve myself and said...I can choose to do this, that, he or she...or I can choose to submit to the will of God totally.

I do believe that there are some that need deliverance in order to be able to make that choice or even come to the resolve of being able to understand your own freedom. But after the houses is swept and clean, it then becomes your job to make sure that the house stays clean. Let's get into some of the discussion regarding deliverance.

So before we even explore deliverance what scriptures, pray tell do we have to even support the notion that deliverance is for a believer. Most of us are used to seeing deliverance in people who are "bound", addicted, gay, alcoholics, etc. But the truth is that we are all living in some state of bondage because we are living in the flesh.

Ok let's go over a couple of scriptures, because I can already feel some people ready to call and get a refund on this book...lol.

Isaiah 61:1-4: The Spirit of the Lord God is upon me; because the Lord hath anointed me to preach good tiding unto the meek; he hath sent me to bind up the broken-hearted, to proclaim liberty to the captives and the opening of the prison to them that are bound. (2) To proclaim the acceptable year of the Lord, and the day of vengeance of our God; to comfort all that mourn; (3) To appoint unto them that mourn in Zion, to give unto them beauty for ashes, the oil of joy for mourning, the garment of praise for the spirit of heaviness; that they might be called trees of righteousness, the planting of the Lord, that he might be glorified. (4) And they shall build the old wastes, they shall rise up the former desolations, and they shall repair the waste cities, the desolations of many generations.

Let's go through some of this and figure out how this has anything to do with inner healing and deliverance. This isn't some weird interpretation. Just follow me.

Starting with the first verse, He has anointed me to preach good tidings or good news to the meek. Meek means to be submissive or to be easily imposed. Why would the person who is submitted need good tidings? It's probable that the person who is meek, or submitted has had to deal with bullies. Yes, the person who is in subjection to someone else or to God has to deal with disappointment at some point because they have chosen to allow

God to be the one that's in control of their outcome! That's a difficult place to be in, especially since we are so used to being in control.

Next he says to bind up the broken hearted. This takes us right in to a definition of what inner healing is. Over the years, my experience has taught me that inner healing is not just about praying for someone, but it is about acknowledging that God is the one that is in control, yesterday, today and forever.

Imagine a tree in front of your house. It would be very difficult to just snatch that tree up out of the ground, without doing a lot of damage of things around it. Inner healing is the shovel that digs around the rocks, the branches and the dirt that clears the debris.

Inner healing sets us up to snatch the thing out of the way that has been keeping us from seeing the sun!!! If we are not healed in an area of deliverance what will typically happen is we will end up back in that same place all over again, trying to figure out, and asking, how did I get here?

What is the process of inner healing? The simple process of inner healing is about allowing God to be God in whatever the area of healing that is needed. It can be seen by some sects of Christendom as too much or not needed...but clearly Jesus came to bind up the broken hearted. He came to put together your broken pieces that your heart has turned into because of the words of people, the cycle of abuse the things that you have convinced yourself were true. This is what He has decided to do for you. He has made it His mission to take your broken pieces, (he is a carpenter), and nail them back together to bring wholeness back to your heart, so that you, being the reflection of Him, can do the same thing in the lives of those that are around you.

For me inner healing dealt with some of the greatest things and some of the smallest things all at the same time. There is not anything too small or too great that God isn't concerned about. He wants to know about it all and fix and mend it all. Someone may be asking, well why doesn't He stop it before whatever that things is hurts me. Well, why doesn't he just have a bunch of robots running around the earth? He has given us the ability to choose to obey. We can choose to disobey, but His greatest desire is that we be saved, He wants us to be in health as our souls prosper.

That kind of takes us to another place. Inner healing is biblical not just with the scripture in Isaiah but also in 3 John1:2, Beloved I would that you would prosper and be in health even as your soul prospers. Your soul is the seat of your emotions, it's your heart. If His desire is that our souls would prosper and be in health, it is then probable that our souls can get sick... No amens?? Ok!!!

These are the facts, we are born, and then we receive our first disappointment the minute we take our first breath and feel that cool breeze. We live 10 months in the secure warm place and now I'm thrust into the atmosphere of cold and people pawing me?

After that, now I have to learn how to find nourishment through eating or drinking? I was just being fed by whatever mother was eating and now I have to use my brain cells to cause my jaws to suck from a bottle or a breast. I have to use my lungs to cry in order to get some attention, and you might not feel moving so I'm allowed to just cry for a little while. Now I have to sit in my own waste as well???? Are you kidding, and then the first person I fall in love with, I realize later is already committed to someone else (that's how I got here). Inner healing goes back this far, or as close in time as, I went to make some coffee this morning and after getting my cup and cream ready, I pour my coffee and reach for the sugar, and can't find a spoon. All I wanted was some coffee. And now I have to pour this sugar into the cup with no coffee. Which triggers how much you really hate where you are in life because you don't have the necessary tools to accomplish what you really want to do?

While we are at this juncture, start forgiving those people that have not had the tools necessary to accomplish what you needed from them emotionally. Some people are just not equipped to do what you need them to do, or be who you need them to be.

The requirements and expectations that we put on people are sometimes full of manipulation and control, on our part. This in itself is not mental illness but a clear demonic cycle or bondage or stronghold that we have kept ourselves in because of the things that we have experienced in life.

I just had the discussion with someone the other day where we discovered that the reason they were responding the way that they were to their own circumstances was because they had made an inner vow. God honors our vows. The issue is this, when we make an inner vow that we will never let anyone in again,

I can't love like that again, I will never trust anyone ever…we make that vow to ourselves. Even when everything in us wants to be loved, to trust or let people in, we can't because our bodies are honoring what we have said with our mouths. The only way to break that is to make sure that you break the vow. Repent to God for not allowing Him to be God and give him that area of your heart again. What will happen if not, is when people come in that we are supposed to trust and build us, we can't and they then become triggers? Red flags go off even when we are supposed to trust them, versus when we are supposed to keep our guard up.

We start to see what is really happening in our hearts during inner healing. An inner vow will cause you to be in love with the perfect person for you and you destroy the marriage from the inside and out of yourself because of the vow that you made to not trust anyone else. This inner vow starts to come out in everything that your spouse does. Every time they come in 10 minutes early or late, you are triggered. You want them to call and text within seconds because of your vow. Sometimes you may try and figure out why you are responding this way when the truth is...you have no idea. The only thing that you really understand is that you can't, for whatever reason, trust anybody.

Once an inner vow is made which can be seen as a seed that we plan in our own souls (seat of your emotions), our entire worlds start to make sure that word comes to pass. There is power of life and death in your words so when you say stuff like: I'm not that spiritual, I never know what God is saying to me, I'm never trusting anyone anymore...when you want to trust, hear God, know what He saying or be that spiritual, suddenly everything gets in the way of you accomplishing anything that you wanted to do, because you made a commitment to yourself and God honors covenant.

I know people will resist this statement but, the truth is that the things that we have decreed and declared out of our mouths come to pass in us or in our atmospheres. Just like the vow you make to the Lord that you will serve Him and you say yes to His will. No matter what comes or goes everything pushes you to bow to His sovereignty. Everything works together...

This is why many people end up in trustless relationships, because you have made a vow in your heart and have committed to making sure that what you have spoken in your heart comes to pass.

Because of this seed and vow, now springs up a root of bitterness, or a bitter root judgment. Because you have jumped to a place and a seat of judgment, everything that is produced in your life is filtered through those judgments and usually you end up becoming that very thing you have promised never to be. That girl that saw an abusive father has vowed to never be in an abusive relationship. This is not a bad thing except when you have promised and worked hard to make sure that are not abused that you then become the abuser. Maybe not physically, but emotionally and spiritually. I'm about to say something that I know is going to upset some people but (shrugs shoulders). The truth is some of the women who are out preaching and pastoring are only doing so because they were suppressed in ministry and therefore had a difficult time breaking out in ministry. For years you have survived and built a successful ministry but have also developed this major control that stops people from getting close to you...especially men. They choose not to serve under anyone. No man is their head and they end up in divorce because they are the pastor...and they are the one that is in charge.

Break the vow. Repent for the vow and allow God to heal that part of your heart so that people won't be eating the fruit of bitterness that you keep giving out.

Back to the question at hand. We need deliverance because we are born in sin and shaped in iniquity. We live in that state, becoming infected by the world, our own thoughts and the devil until a home is made in bondage. Once we give our hearts to Jesus, our spirits now can identify the fact that bondage is not the place where I should be, but some things keep coming up and I know that I need to be healed from them. This my dear, sir and ma'am is a call for deliverance and inner healing.

Let's look at some scripture. There is a scripture that is Listed in the Old and New Testament that discusses Deliverance and inner healing Isaiah 61 and Luke 4. Both speak of the how the Spirit of the Lord is upon me, because he has anointed me to proclaim good news to the poor. He has sent me to proclaim freedom for the prisoners and recovery of sight for the blind, to set the oppressed free.

This is the key scripture we use when it pertains to deliverance and inner healing. Why is this a key scripture? This shows us that Jesus specifically came to do a couple of things. He came to preach, proclaim or make a clear declaration of good news, that things are about to change or that they have changed. To proclaim freedom to the prisoners. Those who have been made captive by other things. When someone is a prisoner they are not taking themselves by force and throwing them behind bars. They are moving in a place that they have been put in and determined ineligible to come out until someone else frees them. This is why Jesus came.

While we are ministering and preaching to the saints about God's grace and living holy; we forget that God came to make us free. The enemy has tried for years to keep us in bondage to our circumstances and issues. He is the one that would tie us by our hands and feet and we not realize that we have been living in a place of bondage. Like the child of a slave. They know nothing else but slavery. Freedom is the thing that is strange and unfamiliar.

As we continue through that scripture we also see the essence of inner healing. To bind or mend the broken hearted. We have all been in a place that our hearts have been broken. Two things happen in these instances. We are either scared to the point we start making vows and bitter root judgments or we realize what the word says about our hearts being broke. Psalms 51:7b says that a broken spirit and a contrite heart He will not push aside or turn away from.

The literal interpretation of that is God respond to the broken hearted and he is drawn to it, clearly based on the other scripture it is to heal the broken hearted.

I remember, one Christmas I purchased a lot of gifts for my kids. I was going through a divorce and I hadn't seen my kids. I wanted to do something that was going to leave a lasting impression on them. I had garbage bags of toys and gifts. My daughter decided to pull one thing from the bag. It was a tan teddy bear with a pink bow on it. She was so excited for that gift. While playing with the other kids I could see her every time she ran by, dragging this bear around with her. After about 2 hours I heard her scream..."Give me my bear". I ran to see one of her friends playing with the bear. I snatched the bear from her and gave it back to my daughter.

Everyone was in an uproar because I took the toy from her. She's a child, they said. Chloe needs to learn how to share. The fact was I heard my daughter's heart break because her daddy gave her something and someone took it from her. I responded to her cry. Then someone gave me wisdom about this too. I responded not just because she was my daughter but because I was daddy. I want my baby protected and covered. When we realize that God has a plan and wants us healed and protected, after we have been through our difficult time, our heart break and our personal difficulties He still wants to heal us. This is where God starts to work in us.

We have a high priest that can be touched by the feeling of our infirmities. We are not just people that are walking around trying to make sure that we are whole.

This is inner healing. This is where God comes to rescue us. He sent his word and healed them. In our inner healing ministry and private session, it is the word that is used to break the control and bonds of the enemy that has kept a person going through the same cycle in their emotions.

Inner healing or healing on the inside is where the pain from the past is healed. We understand that you can never forget, but you don't have to live in the bondage of the past. You don't have to live in the emotional bondage that would plague you and keep you from progressing.

The person that needs (even though we all have been wounded at some point); inner healing is the person that is constantly dealing with the same triggers. The same painful memories keep coming up to torment them.

Inner healing goes to the root of the thing. If you know anything about gardening you understand that in order to pull something out of the ground you have to make sure you pull it up from the root. The only way that you will be able to get it from the root is by removing all the dirt, rocks and sediment that is surrounding it. The stuff that would be there that would get in the way of pulling the root out.

Sometimes we don't realize the stuff that's covering the root of a thing until we start exploring the real issue. This is what inner healing does for you. Inner healing digs beyond all the demonic roots and gets to the said root in order to clearly grasp it and eliminate it.

The inner healing process is what I like to call spiritual therapy. It usually starts out with prayer. Asking the Lord to come in and join a client and minster. This kind of ministry is not specific to the minister but directed to the person receiving ministry. This is not a time to be flashy regarding your gifts, because that person receiving ministry is the one that will be digging through their dirt; you are the one that is handing them the tools.

Before inner healing can take place, even though it's as simple as this, being able to acknowledge that an area needs to be healed. It is one of the worst things in the entire world for people "of faith", to say stuff like: they are not claiming some sickness. The Bible says that Jesus came not for the well, but for the sick. If this is the case, the whole time you have been convinced that you shouldn't "claim" the sickness; you are resisting your healing.

Your experience isn't reality. As a believer, your reality is what his word says. It is what heaven says. If we get stuck in our experiences we will live in a place of bondage to our experiences and not in the reality of life and abundance, which is what was promised by our Lord.

When it comes to inner healing, we have got to recognize our experience but live in the reality of Christ being our healer.

The process for inner healing is not hard, nor is it super spiritual but it is basic and simple, which is why so many people have issues with it. We want it to be spiritual and deep when the work of Christ is actually a lot simpler than we make it. Salvation is just as simple as accepting the work of Christ. We want people baptized, speaking in tongues, laying hands and preaching. The truth is that we need to get to the basic things first. Let's get Him in our hearts first and then add the deep things.

Inner healing is one of the most miraculous and powerful uses and activations of the word of God. It encompasses seeing Jesus as He said He is, the same yesterday today and forever more. Seeing His sovereignty and ability to meet us where we are changes our concept of life and the things we have experienced as well as how we respond to our current situations.

Inner healing is not a fix all. It is not a miracle elixir for Christians. It is a way for us to release the things that we have allowed to hold us in bondage emotionally. My former pastor, Dr. Jerry Piscopo, used to always say that inner healing will not remove the memory but it will remove the pain of the memory. It is a bit like surgery. You are exposing yourself and your heart. That area that needs to be fixed is usually the area that hurts the most and it's never easy to take a look at that stuff, in order to get the chief physician to take a look at it and mend you back together. The fragmented pieces of who you are does not make you a "broken person", it means that you have broken pieces. Every one of us has had that piece of equipment where a button breaks, the volume doesn't work as well or suddenly you have to hit it on the side in order for it to work. The same thing goes for our hearts. We can take the time to throw it out and buy another one...or we can make sure that this particular thing, that we clearly cherish and love, is made whole because it has a broken piece. This is something we must understand as well. The grace of God tells us that even though we have broken pieces we are still viable to be used as a vessel!!!

Again, it is not a fix all; it is a means of ministry and a step of faith in trusting God. It can be seen as therapy with Jesus.

There is a minister that walks with you, but the Holy Spirit is the one that leads the minister and the person receiving ministry. The minister does not ask guided questions but closed questions, while the Holy Spirit brings up memories he wants to heal from.

My first time going through inner healing was great. I sat in the chair across from the minister and he asked me to close my eyes. This made me nervous, because I had to allow my defenses to drop and allow myself to be sensitive and open in front of this person who I do not know. This was a real trust game that God was playing with me.

Why close my eyes. It keeps you from being distracted from the things that are happening around you. Closing your eyes allows God to use your imagination to reflect on your memories. It has been said that those who play video games and watch a lot of TV have trouble allowing God to use their imagination. I beg to differ, it only assisted me, I could be able to visualize a lot more and remember a lot more of my personal memories.

Why do we need visualization? Inner healing deals with the healing of memories, and healing and mending of the emotional brokenness on the inside. This is important because it is the emotional brokenness that sometimes, allows and causes a demonic foothold. This is where we enter the demonic cycles.

Inner healing allows us to see beyond the situation as it is or was and the ability to allow God to heal back then. There was a movie about a guy who went into the past but carried a picture from the present with him. At one point the picture started to fade because he started making changes in the past. This is what inner healing does. If you are healed from the past stuff your present response will be different.

I sat in the chair and closed my eyes as instructed and the minister started to pray: Lord, as we present ourselves to you, we pray that you will allow us to see what you want us to see. Thank you that your word tells us that you are the same, yesterday, today and forever. Thank you that you are in our past, present and future. We invite you Holy Spirit to take control, take my brother to the first memory you want to heal…in Jesus Name amen.

We sat in silence for a few minutes and he then asked, "What is the Lord showing you?" This is important. It was not being led by me or by the minister but by the Lord. It was His job to show me the memory that He wanted to start with. Now, if you are going through inner healing or you're going through this process in your own prayer time. There is nothing wrong with you if you don't see the heavens open up and memories flood back...wait.

Sometimes God will use triggers or prime the pump for us. A smell, a feeling comes over you, a color, a place or something that literally triggers a memory. I've been in an inner healing session where I just saw red. The minister asked me to ask the Lord what does the color red mean, what is He trying to show me? Immediately I heard some middle school kids yelling: Red Ray...Red Ray.

The memory that came up was of me in middle school. Tony was an Italian guy and pretty popular. Even in Jr. High school he had a full mustache and was very aggressive. I wasn't short, but I was very thin (not much has changed since jr high school). He picked on me quite a bit, I have to believe that it was because I was just as popular as he was (probably because I was one of 6 black people at the school), and everyone knew who I was. This one particular day we were outside for gym playing baseball. He was the catcher and I was up to bat. I walked up to the plate swinging my aluminum bat, ready to knock the ball out the park.

The minute I got on base and adjusted my stance, tightened my grip on the bat and raised my elbow, I heard him say: gooooooo Cadillac Lips. I was so embarrassed. It was not just his cat calling, it was that it didn't' stop there. The first baseman yelled out Cadillac lips, then the rest of the team, then people who were in the bleachers started yelling it. I started tearing up. Remember, I was 1 of 6 black people in the school and my sister was one of them. Yes, my lips were big, bigger than all of those that were there, and I knew this. I was already self-conscious because I was black, I was tall and thin and had not grown into my ears or lips and now that's being magnified based on this embarrassing moment.

When this memory surfaced, it was almost devastating to me. I went right back to this place emotionally. I remember smelling the grass and feeling the sun's rays on me. I could feel my blood pressure rising and my hands shaking, everything was so real to me.

I described the entire scene to the ministers and he asked me to describe the feelings I was having. I described each and every one in detail: I was angry, hurt, embarrassed, disappointed in my friends, frustration, helpless and out of place. The minister asked me if I could identify any other things going on in there. I couldn't figure out anything else and then he asked a simple question: Can you ask the Lord if there is another feeling in there that you haven't identified? Just as I was preparing my heart to ask Him, He quickly responded and said self-hatred. I immediately started to cry. I hadn't even considered the fact that my environment had started to shape the view of myself and my own image.

The minister then asked me if I was ready to repent for anything. I was ready. Just like any other issue, that thing has to be identified. I had to address the fact that I went completely against what I knew God thought and felt about me. I sat and repented regarding my ability to believe the words of those that were around me and ignoring His words about me. After that we addressed all the emotions that were explored.

The minister stated that it was important to renounce the feelings that I had given authority to take over. This was an exercise of authority over my own emotions. We have the fruit of the spirit: temperance, we have self-control. I didn't realize that in that instance I allowed for all those emotions to take control of my heart space and create a foot hold for the enemy.

As I sat ready to ask the Lord for the next thing, I was instantly back at that park and seeing what was happening. I was so angry, that I started swinging my bat at Tony. I was so angry and out of control. Suddenly, everyone started saying, "He's turning red". "Red Ray...Red Ray", they all yelled.

I was utterly disgusted all over again. I was so angry and frustrated. I had to repent and renounce the control that those feelings had over me again.

At this point the minister asked me to pause the scene. I started laughing and said how can I pause a memory? He laughed and said, we serve a God of all time, any time and outside of time...yesterday today and forever. Ask God to pause the scene.

This revelation blew my mind. Whatever we have experienced in life, He was always there, before we got there, when we experienced it and after the event.

This is when He asked me to invite Jesus in. I was not too keen on this. We already prayed and identified the emotions that would keep me in bondage. What else is there? I was confused, but trusted what had transpired so far, so why not. How much trouble can we get into asking Jesus to come in? So, I prayed and asked Jesus to come into this memory. As I asked him to come in I pushed play on the memory. It seemed to have started all over again. I was walking up to the mat and I heard Tony yell, Cadillac lips as I tightened my grip, but this time from the bench I heard a voice yell: Knock it out the park. I started to feel myself getting angry as the voices started to rise yelling, Cadillac lips, but I looked out into the field and saw what I believed to be Jesus in the outfield, running back and forth yelling my name.

The peace that I experienced was incredible. It was more than what I expected because of His presence. The minister asked if Jesus wanted to say anything to me. I shrugged my shoulders, unsure of how I was supposed to know. I looked at Jesus and asked Him. He simply said you were made in my image; you were fearfully and wonderfully made. Love all of you like I love all of you.

I was in so much peace. Even now when I think about the memory, I remember the name callings, I remember the feeling of anger and disparity; suddenly the pain of the memory wasn't there anymore. I now remember how even in all of that Jesus was there and was rooting me on the whole time. He is now louder than every other voice in that memory.

The power of those words does not control me anymore. It is as simple as that. His presence really is life changing and heart changing. Even if it is in a memory. Understand that the memory was not rewritten, my perception was changed. I was so focused on looking at all the faces and hearing all of the voices that were yelling all the negative things to me that I wouldn't see Jesus. He was there the whole time.

One of the things that I had to understand is that just like in worship my experience with the Lord is not the same…it's the same with inner healing. There have been times I have seen characteristics of Jesus. I have sensed His presence, seen a light (Jesus is the Light of the world), I have felt a warmth come over me (he's a consuming fire), and the list can continue. But my experience with God in each inner healing moment is different because each memory is different.

As the memories are healed the foot hold is revealed and the cover is pulled off of the demonic, the principality and the stronghold. This gives us the ability to address the demonic activity that has been manifesting in the life of the believer.

There is so much that needs to be covered before the act of deliverance, but it is the simplest things that are ignored. Just like in inner healing, the ability to recognize an issue is always the most important. If you can't be honest, you can't be saved. If you can't be honest you can't be free.

As we explore inner healing we literally put a spot light on the root of an issue, clear the rocks, the dirt and debris out of the way in order for that root to be snatched up and removed so that the person receiving ministry (deliverance) will have the ability to continue in a productive life and increased development in their relationship with God.

It is the inner healing moments that we usually see the cycles of responses in our lives. This is why some of us operate the way that we do. It is not a demon (per se), it is quite probable that it's the manifestation of a wounding and a recurrent response based on said wounding, thus allowing for a demonic foot-hold. This needs to be identified in order for us to make sure we are not blaming the devil for everything. Or giving him power that he does not have. We are the figures of authority in the earth, not the enemy. This is why we can experience deliverance and not be bound by the fact that we are being set free from demonic activity.

Inner healing can and should be done in your private time with the Lord. This does not replace spending time with God, but should be able to be used in addition to spending time in your word, in worship and prayer. You can take time in your time with the Lord and incorporate asking God to heal you in whatever the areas He wants to, in that time.

CHAPTER 4
Deliverance

Alright...now that we have gone through all of the pre deliverance stuff, the time you have all been waiting for. We will cover kids and adults, as well as deliverance for Christians and non-believers.

It has been said before, or at least I have heard it several times that Christians cannot have demons, well...somebody may want to tell all those pastors, prophets, evangelist, apostles and teachers, lay members and several others that have been ministered to, and I personally have cast demons out of them.

The truth is this, yes, a believer can have demons. I'm not just talking based on experience. I'm a believer in the fact that just because you have the experience of it does not make it an absolute truth or reality. It is only your experience. It may be a truth for you but not really an unfaltering truth. The only truth as a believer is the word of God. We are not dictated or controlled by our feelings or our experiences. If you experienced it and it is not supported by the word of God, trust that it is either demonic or soulish.

Anything that I talk to you about regarding deliverance, inner healing, the prophetic or prayer, will always have some sort of scripture (in context) to support my belief system. As it pertains to inner healing, you will have to go back and look at the scriptures that were disclosed there. We are about to explore the scripture that goes over deliverance.

First, how do I know I need deliverance? When you take a minute and realize that you have been going through the same issues over the last couple of years, it's probably a deliverance issue. I was taught years ago that the deliverance or demonic realm is usually seen in the extremes. If you get angry, that doesn't mean you need deliverance that means you need to learn how to respond and get in control of your emotions...lol.

The person that has "anger issues", this one may need deliverance. Do I believe there is a spirit of anger and rage? I believe that the enemy comes to steal, kill and destroy and if the manifestation of that is done through anger and rage, then yes, I do believe that.

So, let's explore one of my favorite scriptures as it pertains to deliverance. Matthew 15:21-28, talks about the Canaanite woman who came to Jesus crying about her daughter. According to this scripture, the daughter came for a specific reason and it was not salvation. This is a great point when it comes to salvation, possession and what church people like to call oppression. The truth is salvation encompasses our physical bodies, souls and our spirit. Jesus died to redeem our souls from death to life. After redemption, we still need salvation in our physical bodies, that's called healing, our souls need to be healed and set free (soul as in the seat of our emotions and our minds).

What does this have to do with deliverance and the believer? Everything!!! This unbelieving believer had enough faith that deliverance is to ask for something that we refuse to believe or adjust to. She asked Jesus for deliverance for her daughter. She specifically said her daughter was vexed, controlled or being tormented by a demon and needed to be free from it. Jesus stated to her that this kind of ministry was designated specifically for those who were believers, the words that he used was His children or the child of the kingdom; those who would be able to receive the inheritance from Him.

This is an issue that goes beyond deliverance. We have an inheritance that has been gifted to us. Most of it is still in the trust because we have not accepted or we have just plain rejected the fact that we can get that part of our inheritance. From the prophetic, healing, deliverance and a host of other things that we have said are not applicable to us anymore.

Truth is, if we can't believe for His grace and gifts we can't receive them and deliverance is a part of that. That's a gift left here for us to live our full lives in the earth. If you don't experience deliverance, will it send you to hell? Absolutely not, but it will give you freedom to live a better life here in the earth.

We already talked about inner healing and the process of that seen in Isaiah. Deliverance is there as well. When we take a look throughout scripture, we constantly see the promise and fulfillment of God's ability to deliver, out of Egypt, out of the hand of the enemy, from the Philistines, from demons etc. The greatest part is that He is always setting us free because our minds are being transformed and renewed by the application of the Word of God.

The bible continues to tell us throughout the gospels about how Jesus gave the disciples power to cast out demons, in Mark 15 the bible tells us that all of Jesus disciples will receive power after the Holy Spirit has come upon them. This is clear that deliverance is a part of the Kingdom. The best part is, back to the scripture that we were talking about when it comes to the women that ran up on Jesus about the daughter.

Jesus response to her was how can I give what is designated for the children to the dogs. He was very direct and specific as it speaks to what is for God's people. She came looking for freedom from demons. Jesus specifically told her that that bread, that gift is for the children not for you.

Eventually they get back into the discussion and she starts talking about how the dogs eat from the masters table. Jesus talks about her faith (basically her persistence and ability to find exactly what she needed from the Master even when He said no), and then he declared that the daughter was free.

Let's not dance around what Jesus was talking about and what we are challenged with. We are always in a place trying to understand how we can be believers and have demons. We question how we can give our lives to Christ and still have or deal with the demonic. How can we have victory and not walk in victory? The truth our perception of life shapes our experiences. This doesn't mean that it's a reality for us.

Let me explain this: Truth in life is that regardless of what we experience in life, we must understand that our experience is not our reality. We are seated in heavenly places and not in the earth. Let me go further. The issue is when we receive Christ, as we explained earlier, our spirit is made alive...but then the next step is dealing with that physical body and that soul. The place where your emotions live and your physical body is where a spirit will hide or live.

Here's something even better. There is no such thing as demons jumping. I just thought I would put this part in here. Nowhere in scripture do we see the bible saying that demons jump. We don't see an example of it at all. Someone will talk about the seven sons of Sceva, but that's not what the bible says, but it is what a lot of people are taught. The bible shows us that it was the 7 sons that jumped on the men and beat them up, it was not the spirits. It continues to amaze me that when it is clearly in our faces we choose to believe exactly what our parents and grandparents taught, out of ignorance. We have gained a lot of knowledge and have the ability to make contact with a lot of people around the world so that we can understand the things that our parents didn't understand. Let's use it.

So, here's something else. Isn't it interesting that demons, when cast out are sent to dry places? And our bodies are 80% water. I used to tell my kids something when they would ask me for something that they "needed". I need those chips, I would respond, you need air to breathe, water to live and Jesus to get to heaven, but you don't need...whatever the thing is.

It's incredible that science and the spirit always somehow prove each other true. I love that it makes sense that in order to torment a demon you remove him from a place that is full of water and send him to the dry places from where he comes from.

Since we are at this juncture, let's look at where demons live and how they are in our bodies and soul. There have been several studies that show that our emotions can affect our physical bodies. That person who is always stressed out can have stomach or ulcer issues. In my experience, when people have extreme physical illness and issues, those can be rooted in demonic spaces that have taken resident in the person's body.

I know...it's a bit much to contemplate and process. I need you to be balanced in this thinking through. Just because you have a cough does not mean that you need to grab some oil and call out the coughing demon. Let me say this as well. EVERYTHING IS NOT A DEMON!!! If you sneeze three times, that is not a demonic attack.

I watched a video of a well-known preacher, and it was so funny to me, that after she had delivered this incredible message, she accidently bumped the camera; mind you it was at the very end of her broadcast. When she bumped it, the camera feel and she had to set it back up. Her response was: "Oh, he mad". "The devil's mad now".

I laughed so hard, and said to myself, that wasn't the devil, that was you. You bumped it. It was because of your action that the camera fell not the working of the devil. It was not in his devious plan to set you up to fail by making the camera fall.

This is something we need to grab a hold of in the body of Christ. The truth is we like to blame our individual actions on the devil because we don't want to take responsibility. I know we talked about this already but, obviously we need to talk about it again. The truth is that we get into a car accident and start to blame the devil. When the truth is you weren't paying attention to traffic and people were speeding, it was the weather or you were doing your makeup, eating or sleepy. The issue is that it was not the devil trying to destroy you. It was life happening.

Now, for things that are demonic, it is our inheritance to be able to receive the promise of freedom from the demonic. Not just demons but from the demonic realm. This includes but is not limited to, principalities, powers, rulers of darkness of this age, against spiritual wickedness in high places. We have the ability and the freedom to get free from all of those things that would ensnare us.

Hopefully we have covered that enough to understand that we can now talk about the process of deliverance itself.

CHAPTER 5
Deliverance –
The Minister and Person Receiving Preparation

The process of deliverance for the minister and the person receiving this type of ministry is really about preparation. Everything that we do in God is always...repeat after me...

EVERYTHING I DO IN GOD IS ALWAYS BASED IN FAITH!!!

Everything that we do is all faith activated. So the first thing that needs to be initiated is faith in the fact that God wants to set you free. Remember that we talked about admitting that you have a problem is the first step in being free? Yeah, you have to admit that there is something that I need to be freed from.

I'm not saying you have to believe in demons inhabiting a believer, but be able to admit, that there may be something else happening in my life that is controlling or dictating my emotions, my responses or the area that I need freedom in. Remember we aren't talking about flesh issues. You know what; sometimes it may be difficult for you to discern if this is a flesh issue or if this is demonic because we are caught right in the middle of it. If it were me, I would have to trust someone else to not just tell me, but the suggestion of the fact that I need deliverance.

My opinion is that we all need deliverance. All of us. Deliverance is my inheritance and I want all that is mine. As the person that is ministering deliverance, it is key to remember that no matter where you sit in doing this ministry, the love of God should be shown to the person receiving ministry. We all need deliverance, even the person doing deliverance. I can already hear people saying I don't want someone who are struggling doing deliverance on me. Well, if that is your answer then you will forever seeking the "sin free" person to minister to you.

The bible says that if we say that we are without sin then we are liars (not sure if you know, but that's a sin in itself). The truth is we all struggle with some issue, and have something we need to be free from. It wouldn't be the children's bread if we didn't need to eat it. It would be designated as "those" children can eat this bread because they need it.

Deliverance isn't a fix all nor is it a measuring stick to say that you are good, perfect or righteous. It is an inheritance to every believer.

As the minister and the deliveree prepares for deliverance the first thing we have to do is understand that we are supposed to do it and receive it. The next step is understanding your authority.

When I first started doing deliverance I watched how others wanted to know the names of the demons that were cast out. As we look at scripture and my personal experiences, I learned, most times it's easier to deal with the manifestation of the said spirit. I can minister to a person based on the actions of the demons. When Paul cast the demon out of the girl that was going behind them, he didn't call out the psychic spirit (to be honest we don't know, and the truth is we only see Jesus casting out a spirit by name or asking for a name one time), he called out the spirit that was annoying him. He didn't have to know the name of the spirit he went by the demonstration of the spirit.

I remember doing deliverance on someone years ago and as we were going through the process of deliverance (calling the spirits out), I ran out of names, and I couldn't see or hear a name, but I kept seeing a cycle of abuse. So, I ran with that, I called out the spirit that would continue the cycle of abuse, and that would be attached to low self-esteem and the feeling of being trapped. I didn't realize it until after they got up off the floor, how attached and associated all of those things were. I realized that my authority goes beyond the basic name of something.

I remember my dad would come home from work and do a walk-through of the house and call all the kids into the kitchen and ask us why isn't the kitchen clean, why isn't the garbage taken out and why is the dining room a mess? His next statement is revelation for us: Get the kitchen clean! Get the garbage out and pick up the dining room. The function of the job was called out and his authority spoke to every person under the sound of his voice. We have that same authority. I don't have to keep yelling at a demon to tell me his name...I don't need to know your name; I need you to know my name and to bow to the authority of Jesus.

The bible says that we shall cast out demons. You will not find anywhere that the bible says that we should try to cast our demons, or the great attempt to cast out a demon will be made.

In preparation for deliverance, the heart has to be ready. Not for the deliverance process itself, but for the recovery and the follow-up. That is the most important part of deliverance, and we will have a chapter specific for that. Understanding your authority in Christ adjusts your heart perception and your behavior as it pertains to receiving and doing deliverance. Sometimes deliverance is seen as it's such a negative thing. The key thing is that if you are looking for that thing to remove the blocks for the flow of the anointing, if you are flowing already and instead of a drip or a trickle you need a gushing of power or if you are looking for the grace to go further than where you are in the presence of God...Deliverance is for you as well.

    The next area that we need to take a look at is going to be fasting and prayer. This kind of goes along with understanding the word and the authority that you have.

The bible says that there are some kind that only comes out through fasting and prayer. We don't really know which those are, thus, you fast in order to remove yourself, get yourself humble to God's power and to have self-control. We don't fast in order for us to have super powers. There are several things that happen because of fasting and it happens because you have taken authority over yourself, not because of the food abstinence. Abstaining from food is great, but if you don't add it to prayer, it's just a hard diet.

As of the writing of this book, I have been in active ministry; I mean preaching and operating in deliverance and the prophetic for 26 years. And it took me about 20 years to understand that fasting is not a magic spell. We treat it as such. You'll hear preachers say, they have to "consecrate" themselves before they preach. The fact is that you should have already been consecrated, set aside and ready for the master's use.

David said he humbled himself with fasting. That's its purpose and that's the reason you fast. You remove the strength of you out of the way and rely on the strength of Christ. We can debate this all day, but let me give you this:

Remember when Jesus was lead into the wilderness to be tempted and he was fasting for 40 days? Was he trying to make sure he came out with power? He was Jesus already, He didn't need to try and get power. What was necessary was for him to bring under subjection the humanity part of him so that divinity could soar and dominate. This is the same thing that is necessary for the life of the believer.

I was told by a friend of mine years ago, that the closer we get to God the more human we become.

It took me a long time to understand that but, I get it now. The truth is that the truth of who we are is manifested the more we look and sound like God. That will only happen if we bring our flesh under subjection.

This is probably why we are told that this kind only comes out through fasting and prayer. Eliminating or subduing the flesh allows for divinity to manifest in you, thus, submitting to the authority of Christ in you. This is the reason for fasting, not to find power…He's already in you.

This is the reason why the person receiving and ministering deliverance is too fast, before and during deliverance. This is not a rule or a requirement, but if you believe in the power of fasting, it is something that needs to be done in this area of ministry.

Do not be afraid. Fear is the opposite of Love and it is the love of God that leads men to repentance. It is because of Love that deliverance is offered to us as believers. If it is not of faith it is clearly sin. We can't operate in faith without love and in fear.

While at the same time let me tell you that there are times we are positioned in an area in deliverance that we have never encountered and we still have to minister to a person. We can be concerned or afraid of how we will deal with the current situation but still be able to "jump in the water".

Understand that we are fighting against demonic spirits, while dealing with people. People are sensitive and are affected by how we address them. So ministers, remember to give comfort to the person receiving ministry and person receiving ministry, remember that they are addressing a spirit, it's nothing personal. Since we are at this juncture, you do not need to ask the spirit its name in order to effectively minister to the person. I know we have discussed this earlier but it is important to remind the minister and the person receiving ministry to PAY NO ATTENTION TO THE NAMES OF THE SPIRITS THAT ARE CALLED OUT. I was taught that many times when people are ministering that because we have stepped in to a supernatural realm, we have been opened to a lot of spiritual activity. With that in mind, sometimes calling out a spirit has to do with its associations, generational stuff, and/or word curses etc.

None of that is the issue, the issue is that we have to remember to believe that God is the deliver and what we are being delivered from is what He wants to deliver us from.

Let's talk about the ministry of deliverance itself. The way that we do deliverance at the altar is different when we do individual ministry. Gathered together in a room, the minister is facing the deliveree as well as 2 other ministers standing alongside them.

As ministry begins, prayer is made by the deliverance minister to cover everyone as well as to be open and led by the Holy Spirit. Sitting across from one another, the minister will make sure that the deliveree is sitting with eyes open. Why is this important? There is absolutely nothing more annoying than to sit and listen to someone run off a list of things. While doing deliverance you want that deliveree relaxed and trusting that you are going to minister to them, and not looking down at a sheet of paper that has demon groupings or a list of things that the deliveree may have written down that they are dealing with.

This is where the faith of the minister is completely activated. In my experience, it is easier to make contact with the person and listen to the Holy Spirit. I have also been at a place where I have been ministering to a person and I literally see something in their eyes. For the person receiving ministry, they may see something in the minister's eyes. That's ok. We all have something that we are dealing with.

This is one of the biggest issues I have seen with people that are in need of deliverance, they either resist the ministry of deliverance or declare that they don't need it; everyone else's stuff is always magnified.

While deliverance is an act of faith it is also very physical. It is one of the few times we can see ourselves take a physical stance against demonic forces. While addressing someone/a demon receiving ministry, a whisper won't do. I'm not saying that you can't whisper and a demon doesn't recognize your authority. What I am saying is...use your authority.

I moved into a house by myself...lol. Not an apartment, but a house. I stayed upstairs and couldn't hear anything going on downstairs. One night I was watching TV, (at the time I had a cat named Sasha Ann), and my cat kept going to the top of the stairs and looking back at me.

Eventually I got up and crept downstairs, there had to be something happening down there.

I came down the stairs through the kitchen and hit the light in the dining room. Half of the body of some guy was inside my house. I stood there for a second in awe. I couldn't believe that someone was breaking in my house. Then I became angry, thinking to myself, how could you not make sure the windows are locked. Then I became angry at him...why are you breaking in my house. I stood there and said...WHAT ARE YOU DOING BRUH!!! I didn't yell, but I spoke loudly and as if there was an intruder that needed someone to let them know that this is not your house sir and you are not free to just come in here.

He looked at me with a crazed look and said: "I'm sorry bro, I thought it was empty, I saw they cleaned it out". I reminded him that I was there and he needed to get out. The next day I called to have an alarm system put in.

What does that have to do with deliverance? My approach to him could have been death and murder; instead I used my vocal authority, realizing that this is my house that needs to be defended. And let him know that even though it has been swept clean, that doesn't mean you have the authority to come in and out as you please. In deliverance, we have to use the same authority.

Tell it to come out! I've used general statements like, every demonic force, that bondage, the principality and power that would keep this person in bondage, I break the cycle of (whatever it may be). I don't' have to know your name; you just need to know my authority. I'll let that soak in for a minute...

Truth is we have been taught and seen on TV when other people have done deliverance that they ask names. Have you ever been in a place and some kids were acting up, and you looked over at them and gave them that parent look? Have you ever spoke to a child that was acting a mess at the mall and told them to listen to their parent and sit down (I do it all the time)? I don't need to know your name; I just need you to be able to recognize my authority and the fact that I am the one really in charge right now. I know you are the loud one, I know that you are doing great demonstrations and have a fit...but after all of that you still have to do what I told you to do, be silent, sit down and come out!!!

When we try to talk to a demon...we will be lied to. It's in your nature to lie, so what else should I expect but for you to lie. Why wouldn't you lie? You're the father of lies, it would be against your nature to not lie, so because I command you to tell the truth that's going to make you go against your nature and tell me the truth?

I don't have any biblical stance for that, that's just my thinking and ideology. A liar is a liar is a liar. So, use your discernment. This is where we must tap into the prophetic area of ministry. You've got to be able to tap into this place where God is giving you what to call you and you're not basing it on what a person believes their demonstrations or manifestations.

Since we have gotten here, another thing that I was taught was NO

MANIFESTATION, NO FREEDOM. All throughout scripture we see some sort of manifestation of a demon leaving or being expelled out of a body. The same is for today. In all my years of doing deliverance I am yet to see a demon be cast out and there is absolutely no manifestation.

Several different manifestations I have seen:

1. Screaming
2. Crying
3. Yelling at you
4. Breathing hard
5. Puking
6. Body Contortions
7. Laughing
8. Fighting
9. Spitting

There are several more that I'm sure you will encounter in your place and time of ministry, but the manifestation is not the big issue. Manifestations happen during deliverance as well as before they are going to come out. There are two issues as it pertains to manifestations and deliverance. Most times they are distractions and try to get you away from the task at hand...casting the demon out. I remember a time when we were doing deliverance and people were manifesting all over the place. Somebody was screaming, somebody barking and one person hit the floor and started slithering like a snake...backward.

Everyone stopped and stared. The focus was completely taken from what was supposed to be done at the moment. They were supposed to be doing deliverance on the people in front of them, but now everyone was looking at this person slithering backward. Our Bishop started yelling...get back to your chairs. It was actually kind of funny. How easily we get distracted by the things that are happening on the outside and the things that are loud. Just because the enemy gets loud doesn't mean that we should change our focus, which probably means that you're on the right track. The moment you're sitting in someone's face and you're doing deliverance and they start responding, that doesn't mean to stop, that means to dig deeper...press in because you're getting on someone's nerves.

As you experience manifestations sometimes they will tell on themselves by their demonstrations. The bible says that you will know a tree by the fruit that it bears. If a tree (demon) is manifesting by gyrating it's probably something lust, perversion etc. Even though these are works of the flesh, there is a spirit that works behind the scene enticing people to participate in the behavior.

The thing is, in the end, the enemy is trying to distract us from the task at hand. Not just in doing deliverance but in our everyday lives. Remember the last time you were at work and somebody just started acting/reacting to nothing? You looked and asked why are they acting like that? It's a demonic manifestation. This isn't God at all, no is it that person, it's demonic and a distraction in order to get you away from the focus you should be on.

When doing deliverance, the most important thing is to remember that you are not the deliverer, you are just a vessel. He has given you authority to "tread upon serpents", but the truth is that He is the one doing the delivering. He commissions His angels, He hastens to perform His word and He works in order to make sure that the words we speak carry power.

What do you do when you have conflict when doing deliverance? Conflict between the other people doing deliverance. There has got to be a lead in any type of ministry. On the prophetic teams that I have been on and lead, it doesn't matter how long a person has been working in that area of ministry, they have to submit to that person who is leading. If they cannot follow the lead, then they should be asked to leave. This in itself is a demonic manifestation, and says with me: THE DEMON DID NOT JUMP!

It is a manifestation of pride that was already in the person that now is manifesting because the atmosphere has been made conducive to deliverance and freedom.

So, as we continue in the act of deliverance, there are several things that can assist you in ministering. Follow the leading of the Holy Spirit. He may lead you to lay hands on the persons' head. Maybe you are dealing with a demon that torments their thoughts; it would make sense to do that. Most of the time, in my years of experience, I have noticed that I would feel lead to lay hands on someone's belly. (If it's a woman, I will have her lay hands and then if need be I will lay hands on top of her hand.) I'll be honest with you. 90% of what you do in deliverance is going to be by faith.

We really don't know why we do some of the stuff that we do. I've seen people wrap and unwrap a person's head with a scarf, because they sensed a "mind binding" spirit...the kind of spirit that won't allow you to think straight or have a clear train of thought. The medical world will call it ADD and/or ADHD. This is not to say that any of these diagnoses are demons, but I am not saying that they are not demonically influenced. I will say that some things are triggered by environment, some are just in us by nature and chemical make-up and the rest are demonic. None of that really matters because if it's broken, needs mending, to be put back together, separated or healed God can do it. The need for deliverance or to experience deliverance is never a bad thing, it's our inheritance.

    I remember a time I was doing an altar call and I was instructed to turn my back on a woman and to just stand there. God spoke to me and told me to do what he says when he says it. I didn't listen. As I stood there he said that he was dealing with the spirit of rejection and abandonment. I just stood there...then suddenly he told me to duck...I questioned, "duck"? Wham, thud...came the punches. I look back like, what the heck is happening back there. So, what I discovered after the service is that for years she has felt like men would turn their back on her and leaves her alone...and even felt like at times, God has and will do the same thing. That triggered a manifestation (no manifestation no freedom!!!).

It was then that I learned two of the greatest lessons in the prophetic and deliverance. There are times that God will use prophetic movement, gestures, actions or words to cause a stirring in an individual, church or environment. The other thing I learned was the ability to listen when God tells you to do something.

Questioning God is not a bad thing...just question as you do what He told you...he might be trying to protect you.

Teams are important as well. You need to make sure you have back up. Is it necessary to have more than one person doing deliverance with you? No, it is not as if you can't do deliverance if you don't have someone working with you, but it's just smart. The truth is Jesus sent the disciples/apostles out in twos. Why would we want to change the way the system is set up. If that is the foundation, let's stick with it.

While doing deliverance in teams it is important to make sure that we know who is leading the deliverance. You don't want to have someone receiving deliverance from 2 different directions. I mean, one person saying spirit of discouragement and the other person saying sprit of rage...figure out who the leader is and back them up. Pray in the Holy Ghost, listen for connecting spirits, i.e. rejection, abandonment etc. or encourage the person in using faith in manifestation. That sounds weird...Let me clarify. Scream with them; if they start coughing, make sure you have some paper towel in order to help them. If they start crying, make sure that you have tissue prepared for them. There is nothing worse than being ministered to by a team that is bickering and fighting, even in silence. You do know you can argue and yell with a look right...So if you are ministering to someone, get over whatever the issue is and deal with the person getting ministry. We can argue and fight later. (Hopefully by the time the ministry has ended you have both gotten deliverance.)

Be able to know when you just don't have it. Be real with yourself. We are all anointed but one plants, one waters but God gives the increase. So, at one time it may be your time to plant and then let them water, and then you can come and water some more. You're not looking for who can get the best response. You're looking to help this person get free and you're working on a team.

If you are working alone, which is never a suggestion from me, unless it is completely necessary, make sure you are not afraid and remember your authority is in Christ!

Deliverance ministry is no a race or a competition to see who can get the most demons to manifest, or who will be the first one to get someone to scream. This is a marathon that needs to be paced. Remember the most important thing anyway; It is not just the prep, it's not just the deliverance. It's always going to be the maintenance. My dad had surgery on his shoulder. The first thing that I said was, "well, how do you think you're going to do with the recovery. That's going to be the hardest part. Not being able to do some of the stuff you're used to doing, and the way you're used to doing them. That's going to be frustrating". This is the way it is in Inner-Healing & Deliverance.

CHAPTER 6
Deliverance – To Children

This is one off the most amazing and scary things I have ever seen and done in my life. Their freedom is amazing and their process is...wow. So, when dealing with infants...yes infants...wrapped in swaddling clothes, laying in their turn tile swings and happy on daddy's chest babies.

This is the best time to start ministry to the babies. Generational stuff you can deal with right from the very beginning instead of dealing with it when they are teenagers. This is where you have to pray and discern and be honest with yourself, if you are doing the ministry to your own baby, (why you would let someone else minister to your newborn but...hey).

I remember taking my daughter through deliverance. She was born in

November and I took her through in December. It was awesome. I held her and we prayed and talked to Jesus about her. I rededicated her to the Lord, I blessed her and prophesied to her and spoke into her future. I even prayed for her spouse and prayed that she would be happy in her relationship as happy as I was the first time I held her.

I began praying in the Holy Ghost, and waited to see or hear what God would say to me. As I prayed and walked she slept in my arms. She was such a peaceful and beautiful baby. I prayed against demonic powers that would try to destroy her. I got to the place where I started breaking generational stuff, and that baby stretched and growled at me, let out a hideous screech and went back to sleep. I said in my mind, somebody better come and get this baby.

There is something that occurs when it comes to dealing with your only stuff…especially with your children. You try to protect your children because you don't want them to go through the same things that you went through. You don't want them to encounter the same stuff that you did. The same hurt, injury, anger, frustration etc.; it has to be dealt with before they make it to the same ages that you did in order to protect them. Why would you keep something like deliverance from them…even if you don't believe in it, what if…just what if it works?

If we are born in sin and shaped in iniquity, it makes sense that we have the ability to come out trapped in the bondage of sin and iniquity, the foothold of the enemy has been established pre-birth.

Deliverance to children is not that much difference than ministering to an adult. The demon is not a child, the person is. How you deal with the child is different but how you deal with the demon is no different. One of small differences is that you don't have to be as aggressive, because the child's heart is already in a submission pose. Humility is already set up for the child because, well, they are a child and have been set up to follow authority.

While ministering to a child it is important to reassure the child that they don't have to be afraid of the demon or the person ministering to them, but celebrate them and encourage their reliance on God. Reassure them that He has all power and God is a good father and protector and has sent his ministers to help the child.

You can also make children's deliverance fun. It's a lot easier to do "mass deliverance" on children than it is on adults. Even as children, they have authority in their mouths. Have the children to make declarations over themselves, taking authority over the footholds of the enemy and over the wiles of the devil. Speak to a specific spirit, and call it out. Have all the kids take a deep breath and just SCREAM (no manifestation no freedom).

I remember doing this for a youth group, which seemed over the top rambunctious. I felt like I discerned a few spirits manifesting. (discernment of spirits is a gift of the spirit not discernment, you can discern anything, and it means seeing the difference between right and wrong. Discernment sees the what, discernment of spirits sees the who). There was some major anger happening in that building so we dealt with it. I got up, told everyone to stand and repeat after me (this was one of the hardest things to get them to do).

Say this: Today... (I repeated and told them to yell it) Today, is the day, I take control. Father, you gave me authority in the earth. I am earth, and I have power over me. I speak to everything in me, not like God and I take back what you took. I am complete, I am whole. Satan, you cannot have a foothold in me. I release and reject the plan of the enemy for my life and my body. Leave me (I told them to get mad and yell it), Leave me!!! LEAVE ME ALONE!!! Now scream!!!!

All of the kids screamed, I told them to yell it again, Leave me alone!! And we finally did it one more time. The final time I had everyone scream. I prayed and dismissed. After I dismissed I walked into my office because I was exhausted from dealing with them. I sat in there for about 3 minutes but I didn't hear a basketball bouncing. I opened my office door, which was adjacent to the gym and they were just kind of standing around. Walked back in to the youth sanctuary and they were just sitting there.

The next week was different. I had parents walking up to me telling me that they didn't know what to do with their kid last week, because they were responsive, listening and attentive. They wanted to know what the bible study was about. I could just tell them the authority of Jesus.

This is the biggest key when it comes to ministering to children; they have to understand that this really is about the authority of Jesus. Nothing else matters. This way they can be encouraged in their gifts and understand that they don't have to be afraid of spiritual things. Kids are more sincere and sensitive to the spiritual realm than we are. They have not been dulled out by the experiences of life and the things happening around them. Their faith and reliance is in the Christ that they see every day and that's their parent and the authority they see in front of them. We teach them who Christ is and about His authority in them.

We show them about his supernatural power and his divinity and ability to conquer anything, even the things that they see in the middle of the night. We have to be able to encourage their gifts and the authority that they have or they will grow up the way that we did. Why leave them curious at every shadow, trying to figure out the supernatural when we are living in it, and so are they. Their dreams are prophetic, they can see angels and in to the heavenly realm. Don't allow them to be afraid of them, let them enjoy the authority of Christ and the authority that they carry because of it.

Be not deceived, God is not mocked, whatever man sows, that shall he also reap. This is the truth even when it comes to our children. What you sow in them as children will be reaped in them as adults. Sow into them faith, trust, dependence and reliance on the authority of Christ and watch the manifestation work in their lives.

CHAPTER 7
Maintenance and Follow Up

This is the most important part of any kind of deliverance ministry. There was a song that recently came out about Fill me up, till I overflow. This is what is needed after deliverance. I'm going to walk through a scripture that we have already gone over.

As previously stated, no matter what kind of surgery that is done, we have to make sure that the maintenance and recovery process is done properly. If it is not done properly we will end up encountering more difficulty and more hurt than the healing that we were searching for.

The person that goes for gastric bypass surgery, that does not follow the prescribed diet and vitamin intake, will end up back in the hospital, sick or even in death. There is a purpose for the prescription that is established for development and increase in strength and recovery. It was and is designed to make sure that your body rest, you suffer as little pain and recovery is done quickly.

If there is no maintenance and follow up of your deliverance ministry, and for the minister you will end up back, asking for help.

Let's take a look at this scripture so that we can walk through the principles of follow up and maintenance after deliverance ministry.

Matthew 12:43-45 King James Version (KJV)

[43] When the unclean spirit is gone out of a man, he walketh through dry places, seeking rest, and findeth none.

⁴⁴ Then he saith, I will return into my house from whence I came out; and when he is come, he findeth it empty, swept, and garnished.

⁴⁵ Then goeth he, and taketh with himself seven other spirits more wicked than himself, and they enter in and dwell there: and the last state of that man is worse than the first. Even so shall it be also unto this wicked generation.

Ok let's start at the beginning. When a person goes through any kind of deliverance ministry the unclean spirit is gone out of the person. The demon walks around through dry places. You never see in scripture a demon being cast out and being sent into "outer darkness, being sent to dry places etc." The minute they are evicted out of a person (who by the way is 80% water) they go directly to dry places. They are in a place of desolation, a place where nothing grows, a place where the need is great and there are very few needs met.

They walk around looking for rest, looking for a place to stand still and quench their thirst and natural desire to steal, kill and destroy and finds none. Demons don't just go out, go into dry places and jump in to someone else, not the way the demonic or the supernatural operates. The ability for the demon to just "jump" on or in even a child demonstrates His ability to not be God and protect his children.

The demon really says, to himself, let me go back to the place I was kicked out of. Remember he was just roaming and looking for somewhere to plant his head, and suddenly remembers that he was evicted from the best place ever. They used to protect me. They even built a huge tower to protect me and I established it as a principality. The demon remembers that he had the opportunity to do whatever he wanted to do that works with is natural drive to destroy something.

The demon gets there he comes in to the house and realizes that the house has been swept clean, put in order and empty. Imagine that. The bible says that the house was swept clean, someone worked to gather everything that was laying around, moved things around and used the tools that they have in order to clean the entire house. At the same time, someone was sweeping someone was setting everything in order. Making sure that things are supposed to be exactly where they are supposed to be. Order has been set and there is nothing broken and nothing lacking.

The interesting thing is the fact that the house is empty. Realize that it's not empty as if there is no couch but empty to the fact that there is no one in authority in the house. There is no landlord; there is no renter there is nothing or nobody occupying the house. The demon thinks: "What in hell am I to do?" Then the demon leaves again goes back to those dry places and tells his friends and cousins that he has found a great place to live. The demon announces to them that he used to live there and because they are stronger, not just stronger, but they are stronger together.

They gather together and head back to the house and make it home. The results are that they are worse than the first. This is the state of the person that goes through deliverance without doing follow up and filling up the house and making sure the strong man stays strong at the house.

Let's go into specific detail. If you go through deliverance and you get set free the tormenters of fear in your mind. Praise Jesus!!! If you go home and continue life the way that you would have before, even as a believer you are still obligated to keep the house clean. It takes continued cleaning, sweeping and making sure that someone is in that house. To stay free. The opposite of fear is love, perfect loves drives out all fear, and we talked about this. Now, if you've gotten free and didn't fill up, fear goes to get rejection, unforgiveness, etc. and now the mind torment that you had before becomes nightmares, and fear of the future and going outside etc.

Check out the grace of God even in this. The demon gets kicked out, comes back to the house, leaves again, gets 7 more and then comes back. Anytime in there, the Holy Spirit can and will speak to us and tell us, replace that fear that you had with love, increase your love meter. Let the boundaries of your heart expand so that I can fill that place. Repent for your apprehension so that you can keep it clean. Continue to be submitted to leadership so that things can be kept in order. I know nobody wants to hear that. Part of deliverance is being able to make sure that someone else can see your stuff and adjust you.

How do you make sure that your house stays swept clean? Stay on your face. Make it your business to be sure that every day is the day that you clean your heart. Check every day, through repentance and make sure that whatever was in your heart is put in place. Allow God to purge you every day of your own individual thoughts and make sure that you exemplify the mind of Christ...I mean you already have it.

The very definitions of sweeping are dirt or refuse collecting. Extending or performed in a long continuous curve or a wide range or effect. Part of sweeping your heart is the impact that deliverance and inner healing should be having on not just you and your immediate family but as well as those that are far reaching. The healing and freedom of the individual heart should impact those outside of your life. The reflection of Christ should be seen in your deliverance.

Making sure that your house does not stay empty. Make the word of God your authority. If the word of God is living, and breathed by Him, it can stand in the midst of us and make sure that we are covered and protected. The word of God says that we are above and not beneath. So, the demon that lies and tells you that you cannot because you are not good enough. Cast that out, and fill it up with the word of the Lord. The level of importance of making sure that we continue to fill ourselves up with the word is immeasurable.

      Prayer and worship is the other way to make sure that that space that has been cleaned and cleared stays clean and full. Being able to spend that time with God and build your relationship with him is going to be paramount in this season. This is going to literally be a matter of life and death. This is the place of decision and being able to see the distractions that WILL come, that will stop you from spending time with God.

It was suggested to me that 15 minutes a day should be suitable. I'm going to suggest 1 hour a day. It doesn't have to be all at one time either. 15 minutes in the morning of worship as you shower and get dressed. Instead of watching the news, put on worship music and worship and pray during that time. While in your commute to work, find out what the traffic says and then play scripture from your phone on the way to work. That's 30 minutes already down, and you're keeping that space filled up.

If you don't journal, start. You can get a wonderful book written a little while ago called, "Behind Closed Doors", and it gives a bit of insight into the prophetic and journaling. It would be beneficial for you in order to see improvement in your conversations with the Lord. Deliverance is not one of those things you get when you go to a regular service and walk away and celebrate. Deliverance and inner healing, both, cause for maintenance.

Be sure to understand that your maintenance is not supposed to be done in fear. I can already hear some people saying, if I miss my 15 minutes during the day, a demon is going to come in. Don't allow the enemy to torment you like that. It is nothing like that. More like, you gaining authority over yourself. You may be wondering too about all the other bondages that you deal with. My former pastor used to always say, you were born in sin and shaped in iniquity. You got saved at 25, and really surrendered your life to the Lord at 28. You went through deliverance at 32. So, for 32 years, you have dealt with some of this stuff. Trust

God to be able to work in and through you to know how to set you free.

So, as you continue your deliverance maintenance, let's not forget a couple of things as well. Some of us will have different kinds of responses to deliverance. For me, it was the most peace I have ever experienced in my life. The very first time I went through deliverance I didn't realize how much chatter went on in my mind. The evening I got home and laid in the bed...I understood what is meant by the peace that surpasses all understanding. I got it!!!

For some of us the joy and exuberance may cause it to be difficult for you to sleep. The level of worship (and if you're in active ministry), the level of insight and revelation you get in the word as well as how clearly you can hear from the Lord...wow!!!

Some of you may experience what is known as "deliverance blues". This is that numbness that you may feel or an emptiness that something has been taken away from you. All of it is temporary, and because we are not a people that are going to be led by our feelings, we understand that it will pass; the good and the bad part.

Know this, that your deliverance and inner healing time will change your life. If you are a believer who does not believe in deliverance, it's ok...it doesn't change its effectiveness but I'm telling you now that if you try it by faith you won't lose anything.

In the end, you want to work with some people that have the ability to work in the area of deliverance ministry. You want to not just deal with people who are good at doing it but who also have fruit that you can look at and say, this person when through and their lives changed for the better.

Remember that wisdom is the principle thing. In deliverance and every area of ministry you must do it in wisdom and in faith. Finally, always remember that:

No Manifestation, No Freedom

Made in the USA
Middletown, DE
03 November 2020